AMERICA AT WAR

WAR OF 1812

Scott Marquette

Rourke Publishing LLC
Vero Beach, Florida 32964

R o u r k e
Publishing LLC

PHOTO CREDITS:
Marine Corps Art Collection: cover, page 8; U.S. Army Center of Military History: pages 6, 16, 32; Defense Visual Information Center: pages 14, 18, 20, 26, 30, 36, 37, 42; National Archives and Records Administration: pages 24, 28, 34, 40; Library of Congress: pages 10, 12, 22, 27; Smithsonian Institution: page 44; U.S. Navy: page 4.

PRODUCED by Lownik Communication Services, Inc. www.lcs-impact.com
DESIGNED by Cunningham Design

Library of Congress Cataloging-in-Publication Data

Marquette, Scott.
  War of 1812 / Scott Marquette.
      p. cm. – (America at war)
Summary: Discusses the events connected with the conflict between the United States and England during the early years of the nineteenth century.
  ISBN 1-58952-389-X (hardcover)
  1. United States–History–War of 1812–Juvenile literature. [1. United States–History–War of 1812.] I. Title. II. America at war (Rourke Publishing)
  E354 .M26 2002
  973.5'2–dc21

                                    2002001239

Printed in the USA

Cover Image:
U.S. troops (in blue) battle the British at the Battle of New Orleans.

Table of Contents

The U.S.S. Constitution, *called "Old Ironsides," became a symbol of America's naval power in the War of 1812.*

*In the War of 1812, American troops fought savage battles
with the British in the frontier wilderness.*

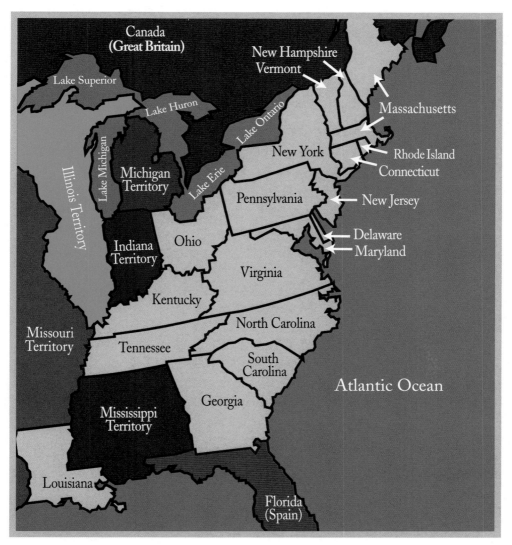

The United States, 1812-1815

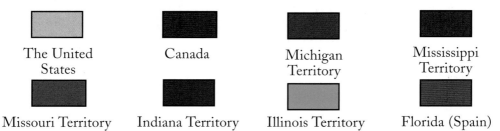

The United States

Canada

Michigan Territory

Mississippi Territory

Missouri Territory

Indiana Territory

Illinois Territory

Florida (Spain)

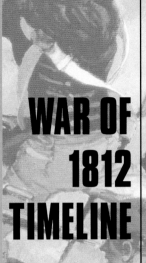

WAR OF 1812 TIMELINE

1807
June: British ship *Leopard* fires on U.S. ship *Chesapeake*

1812
June 16: England repeals Orders in Council

June 18: U.S. declares war on England

August 16: U.S. invades Canada

August 19: U.S. ship *Constitution* captures British ship *Guerriere*

November: British defeat U.S. forces north of Plattsburgh

September 10: U.S. wins Battle of Lake Erie

1813
October 5: Chief Tecumseh killed at Battle of Thames River

1814
March 27: Andrew Jackson defeats Native Americans near Horseshoe Bend

July 25: U.S. forces retreat from Canada after Battle of Lundy's Lane

August 24: British invade and burn Washington, D.C.

September 11: U.S. defeats British ships in Battle of Lake Champlain

September 13: British bombard Ft. McHenry

December 24: U.S. and England sign Treaty of Ghent, ending the war

1815
January 8: Andrew Jackson defeats British troop at Battle of New Orleans

Sea Battles and Indian Wars

In 1812, our country was very young. Just 36 years before, America had fought to be free from England. Many who had fought in the Revolution were still alive. The country was still new. It needed to grow.

Sailing ships were important to the new nation. But American ships were not safe in the early 1800s. England and France were at war. American ships were caught in the middle. The French might **seize** a ship taking goods to England. A ship going to France could be caught by the British. Americans lost more than a thousand ships this way. Because England had a bigger navy, it took more American ships than France did.

England did other things that made Americans angry. Its large navy needed many sailors. British ships stopped American ships and **impressed** sailors. That meant they forced sailors to serve on British ships. They said the sailors were British subjects. But some of the men caught were really Americans.

One day a British ship, the *Leopard*, tried to stop

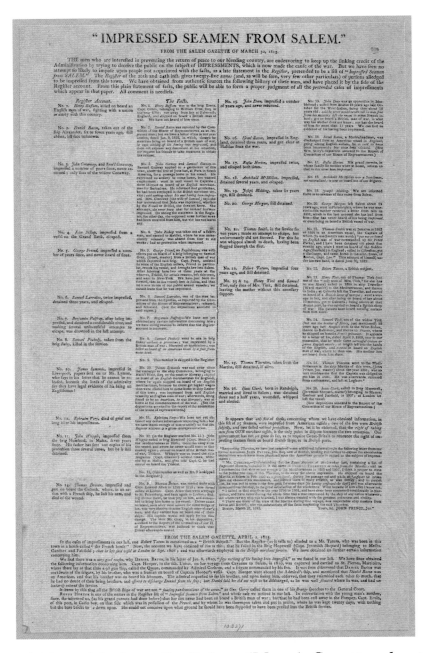

An 1813 article from the Salem (Mass.) Gazette, about the fate of Americans seized by the British. This practice, called impressment, was one of the causes of the War of 1812.

an American ship. The American ship was the *Chesapeake*. The British wanted to search the ship for sailors who had run away. But the captain of the *Chesapeake* would not stop. The *Leopard* fired its guns at the *Chesapeake*. U.S. sailors were hurt and killed. The British dragged four men from the ship. Americans at home were angry when they found out what the *Leopard* had done.

Americans also did not like what was going on in the West. American **pioneers** had moved west to live. They fought with some of the Native American tribes. The tribes did not like the new settlers on their lands. Some Americans thought that England was helping the tribes fight the settlers. They thought England wanted to stop the United States from growing.

James Madison

James Madison was one of the founding fathers who created the U.S. Constitution and the Bill of Rights. He was our fourth president. He wanted to stand firm against England. Some people who did not like the War of 1812 called it "Mr. Madison's War."

President James Madison warned the British to stop impressing American sailors. When they did not, he called for the country to go to war.

By 1811, many people wanted President James Madison to call for war. He warned England to leave American ships alone. He wanted them to **repeal** the **Orders in Council**. This was a law that let the British take American ships. Congress thought a war would come. They passed a law to raise an army of 35,000 men.

England was busy with its war on France. It did

not want to fight another war. England ended the Orders in Council. But the news took a long time to reach America. President Madison did not know the law had ended. He asked Congress to declare war. On June 18, 1812, the U.S. went to war with England. It was just two days after the British had repealed the Orders in Council.

The Constitution *destroyed the British ship*
Guerriere *in less than an hour. It was the first*
U.S. naval victory in the war.

Victory at Sea, Defeat on Land

When the war started, America had only a few warships. The British navy was very large. It had won many sea battles with France and Spain. So it was a surprise when the U.S. started capturing British ships!

In August, an American ship called the **Constitution** destroyed the British ship **Guerriere**. The fight took just half an hour. One of the shots from the British ship bounced off the side of the *Constitution*. After that, the sailors called her "Old Ironsides."

A few months later, the *Constitution* caught another British ship, the **Java**. The ship *United States* defeated the British ship **Macedonian**. Victories like these excited Americans.

But on land, the war did not go so well. The U.S. tried to **invade** Canada. Madison wanted to stop the British in Canada from helping the native tribes. He also thought he could add more land to the United States. In July, U.S. General William Hull led a small band of troops across the border into Canada. It was in the area that would one day be the state of Michigan.

American troops had to deal with many Native American tribes on the frontier. Some tribes helped the British in the early days of the war.

British and Canadian soldiers, fighting with native tribes, forced the U.S. troops to pull back. They even made General Hull abandon Fort Detroit. The British then moved their troops into Ohio—right on to U.S. soil. The U.S. lost control of the **Great Lakes**. Only British ships could move there safely.

On land, America faced a problem. Its army was small. The army needed the help of local **militias**. These were groups of men who volunteered to help fight for a short time. But the men in the militias were not like normal soldiers. Sometimes they did not follow orders. They fought when they wanted to. Sometimes they went home early.

Later that year, American troops tried again to invade Canada. This time they crossed the Niagara River in western New York. But the force was too small and the militia would not come to help. The **invasion** failed.

The same thing happened when General Henry Dearborn led a third invasion. His troops crossed the border near the town of Plattsburgh, New York. Once more, the militia

War in the Wilderness

Soldiers fighting in the West and North had a hard life. When the British held the Great Lakes, food was very scarce because ships could not bring it. Hundreds of men died of hunger before they ever fought a battle.

*The U.S. won many battles at sea in the early days of the war.
The tiny new navy fought with spirit and courage.*

would not join the battle. They said they could not be ordered to leave the country. The small U.S. force was defeated.

As the first year of the war came to an end, some

Americans were discouraged. The navy had won many battles. But the army had been beaten over and over again. And British troops were on U.S. soil. But the worst was yet to come.

Commander Oliver Perry abandons his ship during the Battle of Lake Erie. The U.S. fleet hung on to defeat the British and take control of the Great Lakes.

"We Have Met the Enemy"

The British were stung by the American victories on the sea. In 1813, they sent more warships to block U.S. ports. The **blockade** was meant to stop any ships that tried to bring goods to or from the country. The loss of trade made life hard for Americans.

Even worse, the U.S. lost the *Chesapeake*. The ship became famous after it was fired on by the *Leopard*. In June, the captain of the *Chesapeake*, James Lawrence, went out to fight a British ship, the ***Shannon***. But he had a new crew that did not know how to fight well.

The *Shannon* captured the *Chesapeake*. Captain Lawrence died in the fight. Before he died, he told his men, "Don't give up the ship!" His last words were a motto for Americans who were angry and sad at the loss of the famous ship.

On the Great Lakes, the news was better. The U.S. built a new **fleet** of warships on Lake Erie. They wanted to take back control of the lakes, so they could send supplies to soldiers fighting in the West.

General Andrew Jackson fought many battles with Native American tribes who were helping the British.

Commander Oliver Perry took the new fleet out to meet the British ships on Lake Erie. There was a huge battle. The Americans lost some ships, but hung on to win the fight. The U.S. captured the whole British force and took control of the Great Lakes. Perry sent out the famous message, "We have met the enemy, and they are ours."

The victory on Lake Erie was important. The head of the British troops in Ohio learned that America was now in control of the Great Lakes. He moved his troops back to the Niagara **territory**. This gave the U.S. a chance to try to invade Canada again.

General William Henry Harrison took his troops across Lake Erie. He attacked the British at the Thames River in Canada. This time, the U.S. forces won. The great Native American chief, Tecumseh, died in the battle. He was leading his warriors to help the British.

Andrew Jackson

Andrew Jackson was famous for his battles with Native Americans. He was called the "Hero of New Orleans" because he beat the British there. He was so well known that in 1829 he was voted president.

After winning the Battle of Lake Erie, U.S. forces crossed the lake and defeated the British at the Thames River in Canada. The great Native American chief, Tecumseh, died in the battle.

In October, General James Wilkinson took a force of 2,000 men from Sackets Harbor, New York, into Canada. He did not get far. The British troops beat his men back. A second force of U.S. troops was supposed to come from Plattsburgh. They heard about the fighting and pulled back instead. The British kept marching. They moved into the U.S. and burned the towns of Black Rock and Buffalo, New York.

In the South, General Andrew Jackson was fighting

against the **Creek** tribes. These tribes had killed American settlers in the Mississippi territory. The British encouraged the Creeks to fight the settlers. In March of 1914, General Jackson's troops caught a large band of Creeks. The soldiers killed many of the Native Americans in the battle.

For Americans at home, the invasion and burning of Washington, D.C., was one of the worst moments of the war.

America in Flames

Many Americans suffered during the war. Because the British were blockading U.S. ports, prices went up. The cost of things like tea and sugar went so high people could not buy them.

Manufacturers could not get the raw materials they needed to make products. They could not sell their products in Europe. Many people in cities lost their jobs. Farmers had a hard time, too. They had fewer places to sell their crops.

The hard times made many people wonder if the war was a good thing. The northeast states relied on shipping. Many people there called for an end to the war. But others thought it was their patriotic duty to support the war. Sometimes fights broke out between those who were for the war and those who thought it was wrong.

First Lady Dolley Madison stayed behind after her husband fled Washington, D.C. She saved important papers from being destroyed by the British.

ANOTHER GLORIOUS VICTORY.

NEWPORT, Oct. 18, 1813.

THIS afternoon arrived in this harbor the British Packet MORGIANA, Capt. Cunningham, of 18 guns, and 50 men, prize to the privateer Saratoga, Capt. Addington, of N. York. The Morgiana sailed from Falmouth 27th. Aug. with the mail for Surrinam, and was taken on the 26th Sept. off Surrinam Bank, by the Saratoga after an action of one hour and 5 minutes, by boarding. The following is an extract from the Saratoga's journal :—

"Sept. 21, commenced with light winds, and fine weather ; at half past 5 A. M. saw a sail on the weather bow ; made sail in chase— at 3 P. M. she hoisted English colors, and commenced firing with her stern chasers : At 3 : 20, P. M. the action commenced within pistol shot, and continued till 25 minutes past 4, when we carried her by boarding. with the loss of our first Lieutenant, and one man killed, and 6 wounded, one of them mortally. The prize proved to be the King's Packet Morgiana, of 18 guns and 50 men, from England bound to Surrinam. Her loss was two killed, and 3 wounded, five of them mortally—among the wounded is Capt. CUNNINGHAM, and the first offi- cer of the Packet. The quarters of the Morgiana were superior to those of the Saratoga."

OLD Neptune, the God of the ocean one day,
To Columbia's fair genius did pleasantly say,
Your sons on my waters have made a great noise,
And I'm sure your'e a parcel of fine spunky boys.
CHORUS.
The trident of Neptune in future they'll wield,
And conquering ride on the blue wat'ry field.

The genius replied, Of my sons I'm quite proud,
Their glory is bright, nor is stain'd with a cloud,
And they ne'er shall disgrace of their country the name,
But shall fill with their deeds many pages of fame.
The trident of Neptune in future they'll wield,
And conquering ride on the blue wat'ry field.

While thus they were chating, a terrible din,
At a distance aloof, was there heard to begin,
They turn'd, and two vessels just then hove in sight,
Hot, hot, was the fray, and loud rag'd the fight.
The trident of Neptune, in future they'll wield,
And conquering ride on the blue wat'ry field.

Says old NEP. by the smoke which I now see that way,
I'm sure that the devil himself is to pay,
Let's go to the scene of the battle and see,
Which ship is most worthy the favor of me.

The trident of Neptune, in future they'll wield,
And conquering ride on the blue-wat'ry field,

Away then they fled, but the battle was o'er,
The streamers of George was again forc'd to lower,
And Columbian's bright Eagle, once more was dis- play'd,
Perch'd high on the proud Morgiana's mast-head.
The trident of Neptune in future they'll wield,
And conquering ride on the blue wat'ry field.

On the conqueror the God of the ocean then smil'd,
And pronounc'd him to be of true valor a child,
Then order'd his Tritons a garland to weave,
And bind with the halo the brows of the brave.
The trident of Neptune, in future they'll wield,
And conquering ride on the blue wat'ry field.

Now success to the tight little smart privateer,
Who went to the battle undaunted by fear,
And the fine *Saratoga* which sails on the sea,
Shall as famous as old *Saratoga's* plains be.
The trident of Neptune, in future they'll wield,
And conquering ride on the blue wat'ry field.

☞ PRINTED BY N. COVERLY, Jun.

Popular songs and poems about the war helped
keep people's patriotic spirit up.

Many men went away to fight in the war, so women had to take over their jobs. In the 1800s, most people thought women should stay at home. But with the men away at war, women ran farms and shops. They also went to live at the army camps, cooking and taking care of wounded soldiers.

The worst thing about the war was that Americans were afraid. Settlers who lived in the West feared being killed by Native Americans. People who lived in the East were afraid of British soldiers who burned their towns and homes. It was as if the enemy was right at their door.

The most terrifying moment came when the British burned the nation's capital. In August 1814, they landed 3,500 troops in Maryland. They marched to destroy Washington, D.C. There was not much to stop the

Doing Without

With no ships to bring goods from across the sea, Americans had to make more things for themselves. Instead of imported wheat flour, they used corn flour. They made clothes out of rough, homespun wool cloth instead of fine cotton cloth from England.

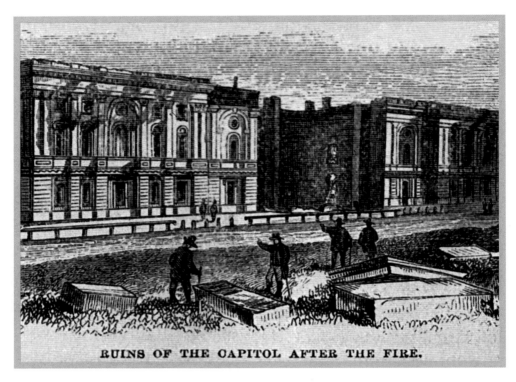

RUINS OF THE CAPITOL AFTER THE FIRE.

The British invasion of Washington left the Capitol building in ruins.

British. A small group of sailors and Marines fought as long as they could. But most of the militia ran away.

President Madison and other officials grabbed important papers and fled into the country. The president's wife, Dolley, stayed longer. She saved the **Declaration of Independence** and a famous portrait of George Washington. Then she left the White House.

British troops burned the Capitol and the White House. Soon much of the city was on fire. People panicked and ran for their lives. The next day the British just sailed away.

General Winfield Scott leads U.S. troops in the Battle of Chippewa. The British were surprised at how well the Americans fought.

The Mistaken Victory

In 1814, the British decided to send more forces to America. They were winning their war with France. That meant they had more ships and soldiers to fight in the New World.

But the armies of the U.S. were learning to fight well. General Winfield Scott trained a force of 3,500 men to fight on the Niagara frontier. In July, he fought the British at Chippewa, near Niagara Falls. The British troops were surprised at how well the American soldiers fought.

The British sent more troops to the area. At Lundy's Lane, near Chippewa, the two sides fought a major battle. Many soldiers were killed. The U.S. troops pulled back out of Canada.

In September, a large group of British ships attacked a smaller U.S. fleet on Lake Champlain in New York state. Captain George Downie commanded the U.S. ships. After a two-hour fight, it looked as if the Americans had lost. But Captain Downie's ship hung on, and the British fleet was defeated. British land troops in the area heard about the loss. They pulled back into Canada. The Battle of Lake

In September 1814, the British attacked Fort McHenry at the mouth of Baltimore harbor. The soldiers at the fort refused to surrender.

Champlain was a major win for the Americans.

In Maryland that same month, British ships fired **mortars** and rockets at Fort McHenry. The fort guarded the entrance to Baltimore harbor. The attack went on all day and night. But in the morning, the men in the fort did not give up. The British had to give up the attack.

While the war went on, British and American officials met at Ghent, in Europe, to talk about peace. The British wanted to stop the growth of the U.S. The Americans wanted England to pay for the ships it had taken. It also wanted the British to stop seizing sailors from U.S. ships.

But both sides had tired of the war. In the end, the two sides just agreed to stop fighting. On Christmas Eve 1814, they signed the **Treaty of Ghent**. The treaty ended the war. But there was one more battle to be fought.

In January of 1815, the British attacked New Orleans. The town was important. It guarded the mouth of the Mississippi River. The British did not

"Rocket's Red Glare"

In the Battle of Fort McHenry, the British used a new weapon. It was called a Congreve rocket. The rockets could be fired from ships. They were not very accurate, but they scared enemy soldiers.

The British and the U.S.
signed the Treaty of Ghent on Christmas Eve, 1814.
The treaty ended the War of 1812.

know the war was over. They landed a force of 8,000 troops. They attacked a fort commanded by General Andrew Jackson. He had only 5,000 men.

The British charged the fort. The Americans fired their cannons. About 2,000 British troops were killed in just 25 minutes. The British gave up the attack and sailed away. It was a major victory for the Americans.

General Jackson became a national hero for winning the Battle of New Orleans. He would later become president.

"Don't Give Up the Ship!"

When the War of 1812 ended, Americans celebrated. Many people felt the country had won a great victory. The U.S. had shown that it could stand up for its rights. It had fought one of the world's great military powers and stood its ground. At last, England treated the U.S. like a free nation. People felt **patriotic** and proud of their country.

At the same time, many Americans were tired of war. They were not eager to fight other countries. Many people felt the nation should think more about its own business at home. The U.S. has been at peace with Canada ever since.

With the coming of peace, the country now had room to grow. The British no longer encouraged Native American tribes to fight the pioneers. Settlers moved into Florida and into the lands near the Mississippi. The U.S. economy also grew. Its ships were once more free to sail the seas. Prices of imported goods went down. Sales of U.S. goods in the rest of the world went up.

Washington, D.C., which the British had burned, was rebuilt. A new White House and the Capitol

The Capitol building and many other public buildings were painstakingly rebuilt after the war.

building were constructed. The buildings still stand today.

Many of the heroes of the War of 1812 went on to lead the country. Voters chose Andrew Jackson to be president in 1829. William Henry Harrison won fame when he beat the British at the Thames River. He won the vote for president in 1841. A young officer in the war, Zachary Taylor, was elected president in 1849.

Many songs and sayings of the war still live on today. People still say, "Don't give up the ship!" when they want to encourage you to keep trying. And a famous song of the day became our national anthem.

A young American named Francis Scott Key watched the bombing of Fort McHenry from a British ship. All through the night, Key was afraid that the men in the fort would drop their flag, to show they wanted to give up. But the next day, the flag was still there.

Chief Tecumseh

Chief Tecumseh was the chief of the Shawnee, a tribe that fought on the side of the British. He was a respected and feared leader. When he died, many Shawnee would no longer fight. It was a blow to the British war effort.

Captain James Lawrence's dying words during the capture of the Chesapeake—*"Don't give up the ship!"—have become a national slogan.*

Key was so happy and proud he wrote a poem. The poem soon became a popular song. The song was "The Star-Spangled Banner." It was named after the new U.S. flag that flew over the fort. Through the years, the song has made Americans remember the bravery of the men who fought to defend the nation. In 1931, Congress made the song the national anthem of the United States. Today, almost 200 years after the War of 1812, we still sing the words

> *O say does that star-spangled banner yet wave,*
> *O'er the land of the free and the home of the brave?*

The flag that flew over Fort McHenry inspired our national anthem, "The Star-Spangled Banner."

Further Reading

Buckley, Sarah Masters. *The Smuggler's Treasure*. Pleasant Company Publications, 1999.

Connell, Kate. *These Lands Are Ours: Tecumseh's Fight for the Old Northwest*, Steck-Vaughn, 1993.

Gay, Kathlyn. *War of 1812*. Twenty-First Century Books, 1995.

Gillem, Harriette. *Washington City Is Burning*. Atheneum, 1996.

Quiri, Patricia Ryon. *The National Anthem*. Children's Press, 1998.

Weitzman, David. *Old Ironsides: Americans Build a Fighting Ship*. Houghton Mifflin, 1997.

Whelan, Gloria. *Once on This Island*. HarperCollins, 1996.

Websites to Visit
Documents of the War of 1812
www.hillsdale.edu/dept/History/Documents/War/FR1812.htm

USS Constitution Museum
www.ussconstitutionmuseum.org

Glossary

blockade — use of ships to keep goods from entering or leaving a country

Congreve rocket — a missile launched from ships

Constitution — a U.S. warship, also known as "Old Ironsides"

Constitution — a document that sets the rules for a government

Creek — a Native American tribe that lived in the Mississippi territory and fought on the side of the British

Declaration of Independence — document that declared the colonies a new nation, free from Britain

fleet — a large group of ships

Great Lakes — a chain of major lakes stretching from New York to Minnesota; they include Ontario, Erie, Huron, Michigan, and Superior

Guerriere — a British warship, captured by the *Constitution*

impressed — someone forced to serve in the British navy

invade — to move troops into an enemy's country

invasion — to invade a country

Java — A British warship, captured by the *Constitution*

Macedonian — a British warship, captured by the U.S. ship *United States*

manufacturers — companies that make things, often in a factory

militias — groups of people who agree to fight only for a short time when needed

mortars — special guns that fire shells that blow up after they land

Orders in Council — a British law that made it legal for British ships to stop ships from other countries

patriotic — a feeling of being proud of your country and wanting to protect it

pioneers — the first people from a group to move into and live in an area

repeal — to end a law

seize — to take something by force

Shannon — a British ship that captured the *Chesapeake*

Shawnee — a Native American tribe that lived in the Ohio region and fought along with the British

Tecumseh — leader of the Shawnee tribe

territory — an area of land that has not yet become a state

Treaty of Ghent — the paper in which the U.S. and England agreed to end the War of 1812

Index